NAVIGATING YOUR (LOVE) LIFE WHILE QUEER & BLACK

A User Guide to Interracial Relationships

Méfiré

DEDICATED TO:

Charlotte, Amber and Neusa

who have been a tremendous support during this unprecedented time and who helped me keep my sanity.

Mum,

With all my love.

PREFACE

I have always wanted to write a book; I have mostly written poems but also an autobiographical novel when I was way younger. I have never followed any creative writing courses and English isn't my first language, so you might think that I am aiming too high and you are probably right.

I am not planning on writing the book of the year nor the best seller that everyone will talk about. Instead I am just sharing my experience, in the hope that it might help some of you.

Moreover, I am a poet and I have dreamed several times of publishing a poetry book, so I have combined both in this project. Therefore, you should find some of my poems here and there, which will be linked to the theme of the section, a bit like how you would add illustrations to a children's book.

I cannot believe I've written it down, overcoming this imposter syndrome that has been following me during all these years. Yes, Méfi, you write poetry – therefore you are a poet!

I may have lost myself a bit and you must wonder where I am going, what point is she trying to make? Before I explain the purpose of this book or essay, I want to make a promise to myself and to you readers that I will always stay true to myself throughout this book. I will probably unpack things I have never thought or said out loud before, and even if it might feel uncomfortable from time to time, I want to do it. It's part of the process, isn't it?

Let the show begin, then. So, I guess it all happened after this latest breakup. It will sound a bit ridiculous because I only dated this person for four months, though we had a deep connection. We also dated in 2018, but it did not work out. It was like those undeserved, impossible love stories, like a *Romeo and Romeo* Shakespearean tragedy. Sounds dramatic… and it was!

After dating Hector for four months (name changed to keep anonymity), I decided to end our relationship because I kind of lost myself in it. I am saying this now but I'm still trying to figure out if it was the right decision. To be totally frank, if you ask me now on the spot, I will tell you that I am deeply suffering and I miss them a hell of a lot. It feels like I made a mistake and got caught up in the moment, overwhelmed by my emotions and a bit hopeless for the future of our relationship. It is complicated because there is love involved. I love them so much, and I am wondering if they do too, or at least feel something on a similar level.

Nonetheless, I have tried to turn the breakup into something positive, to take it as a moment for introspection, and writing has been part of the healing process. What I have unpacked so far is that before Hector, I was in a year-and-a-half relationship with a cis white woman called Julie (name changed to keep anonymity) which deeply damaged my sense of self because I had to repress my Blackness. After eight months in this relationship, I consciously chose not to bring up any discussion about race because I knew she'd just shut down or I would get the usual 'not everything is about race' excuse thrown in my face.

I almost jumped straightaway into a relationship with Hector, while still navigating through the horrendous breakup with Julie. While I knew I wasn't feeling anything for Julie anymore, despite our year-and-a-half relationship, I realized later that I still needed closure. How was I meant to close this chapter if I was not allowing myself to process my emotions, to 'cry it out' as we say, to cleanse and to centre?

When the relationship with Julie ended, I decided to keep the flat we were renting because it was the most convenient and wise thing to do – not financially though – but we had signed a contract until November and the breakup happened in May. She could not afford to keep the flat, so I decided I'd do it because it was the only way out, as cohabitation was not an option. We did have to coexist under the same roof for two months, which was unbearable. I often wonder how people (myself included) who used to love each other can reach a point when they cannot be civil to one another anymore or even feel hate toward each other.

So today, I am Day 3 post-breakup with Hector, and I struggle. Not everything was lovely, of course, otherwise I would not have taken that decision, but I do feel like I did not give us enough time. I kind of regretted my decision straight after I said it. I messaged Hector the next day to tell them I missed them and that I would like us to have a discussion. Unfortunately, Hector said they needed some space to process things because it was all confusing. I agree, Hector, it is a mindf*** for me too!

To fill you in, years ago in 2018, when Hector and I used to date, they acted in a confusing way too, by not really knowing what they wanted. They would say they want to be with me, but then the next day would choose to go back to their ex. A *'je t'aime moi non plus'* situation, we call it in French – literally translated as 'I love you me neither'. Pretty self-explanatory saying, don't you think?

Anyway, today I was in their shoes, the shoes I had so often criticized, those shoes that made me feel weak, insecure, not good enough – yes, those ones: appealing and tight shoes.

They said to me once via a message on Instagram that they thought we were both suffering from fear of abandonment. I think they were right. I ended things with Hector, preventing them from doing it first, because I was scared they would leave me one day, to look for a greener non-French grass somewhere else.

I was scared. I was scared, I was not attractive-interesting-loving-funny-charming-smart enough. But also, I was not white enough. Beauty standards say you must be white, cis, not too tall, skinny, and have long or mid-long straightened hair, but I wasn't all of that – I am not and will never be. I could not stop comparing myself to their exes, who were luckiest because they could at least tick several boxes from this elitist list. I imagine you can sense how my previous relationship with Julie also came to feed this narrative. Keeping the above in mind, who is responsible for breaking the narrative in an interracial relationship then? Is it the role of the Black person to overcome their anti-Blackness demons, or is it for the white person to make their Black partner feel loved and desirable? Perhaps it is a dual responsibility, isn't it?

I wish I had a user guide to give to white folks dating Black folks on how to manage and challenge unbalanced racial power dynamics in romantic relationships. I wish there were a user guide for romantic interracial relationships. I wish I had a guide explaining to me how to navigate both gender and race, in an unbalanced cis-nonbinary-Black-white relationship.

I wish I could use a guide to help me navigate my OWN feelings, as a Black queer woman going through a breakup, especially because breakups are tackling our self-worth, triggering a forever feeling of being invisible and ignored by the rest.

So I googled it, desperately looking for help – even a few pages would do. Today was not the only day I'd looked for it in vain. This miraculous book, a grail that I would have perhaps found on the twentieth page of my Google search, a guide called *How to Navigate Your (Love) Life While Queer & Black*.

Summary

CHAPTER 1

Building a Strong Foundation

I have been dating white people more than Black/PoC folks my entire life, and this is definitely due to internalized anti-Blackness. I am 31 years old, and I would say I have spent eight years of my dating life dating cis white men, and for the seven remaining years, queer folks.

Before I realized I was queer, I never really questioned myself, because I also did not realize I was Black, on a political standpoint. By saying this, I mean I knew I was Black, because it's obvious visually, but I did not know clearly what impact being Black had on my life. I evidently linked Blackness to the concept of racism but without linking it so much to whiteness. I can understand now how both are connected and how talking about anti-Blackness without mentioning the concept of whiteness is putting the responsibility on the victim and not on the oppressor. Furthermore, I also recognize now that what I called racism back then was, to be more precise, micro-aggressions, which I would define as an active but mostly unintentional tool to spread racist hate.

At the time, I remember I was one of those people who would say I never really experienced racism. I denied what I was going through. I was thinking things like, 'It's fine', or 'It's just a joke', or people wanted to touch my hair because they were intrigued, or I found it funny, and thought, 'That's no big deal!' I thought that racism meant being physically assaulted. I saw it as something extreme, full of visible and tangible violence. Wouldn't it be easier if racism were only that?

Systemic racism is vicious. It often gives me vertigo because it is so ingrained in society, hence it is sometimes almost impossible to detect it or to separate it from the status quo. But if you can't detect something, how can you address it?

I learnt recently from Sabah Choudrey, a queer Pakistani activist writer and speaker who inspires me a lot, the notion of anti-Blackness and how it better fits the narrative than using the word 'racism' when addressing racial discrimination towards Black people especially. This approach made total sense to me; indeed, racism encapsulates so many things and is now often used incorrectly as an umbrella term to describe diverse types of discrimination, or is often used interchangeably with the word 'xenophobia'. We have also seen the example of 'reverse racism', as if racism was somehow easy to copycat and was not the result of years and years of oppression. Because anti-Blackness is insidious, it implies that work must be done from within to then influence more widely. So, work must be done on smaller scale, firstly within ourselves, then within our support system such as our chosen/family, social and work environments, to then reach a wider scale such as society.

Furthermore, as a Black person being able to spot anti-Blackness means you'll be able to mitigate the impact it has on yourself, and therefore reduce mental exhaustion. We often talk about how it is important for white folks to educate themselves, but on a personal level, I have seen how beneficial it was to increase my own knowledge on race and gender. When I began educating myself on racial issues, I finally awakened; I was able to understand my own feelings, understand my struggle and to some extent the struggle experienced by other Black folks. There is a long way to go and it requires energy and an open mind, but it is worth it. That's why, after undertaking this long and never-ending assignment of unpacking and unlearning anti-Blackness, I refuse to go back and excuse myself for being Black anymore. You will see me wearing my 'Unapologetically Black' badge frequently nowadays.

<u>Work must be done!</u>

White folks dating Black folks, you are expected to do better and learn faster.

It's kind of part of the deal, right? It is not an easy mission – I understand. However, don't you want to give your partner the respect they deserve? Don't you want to be a better person? Great, but what does this mean concretely?

It means that in order to do so, you must challenge your whiteness; you must challenge your reactions, your behaviours, analyse your emotions and your thoughts. And how do you do that? By educating yourself – we simply cannot say it enough. The good thing is that after a certain point, you will retain the information and your brain will get conditioned to question things automatically. It's similar to the *non-awakening process*: because of years and years of whitewashed education at school but also from the media, your brain has set whiteness as default. Therefore, you won't ask yourself why there are no or few black people in a mainstream TV program or movie because everything you see or touch is like that. It is the norm – whiteness is the norm.

So once you start educating yourself, you will start questioning the status quo, simply because the new information you've learned is different from what you've been told all your life. After a little while, you'll unconsciously or even involuntarily start unpacking anti-Blackness – not just your own, but also others'. Your mind will wonder, 'Is this thought biased?', 'Was what they said racist?', 'Is this behaviour of mine influenced by my own anti-Blackness?'

It does sound amazing, like a superhero capable of seeing through things and detecting the truth, but even if it does seem like a wonderful power to have, it is also unfortunately a curse. Indeed, being able to understand the real meaning of things does hurt, as it also means that you will overthink and overanalyse almost certainly every situation you are in. Nevertheless, in order to reach this level of awareness, you must do the work for a little while. Moreover, your intentions and interest must be genuine; that's the only way you will actually be able to learn and evolve.

That's why before beginning this learning, you should do a self-check and ask yourself what your intentions are, and why you are willing to do the work. This way, you will keep reminding yourself why the energy you put in is important and necessary. I believe it's important to know our purpose, and why we are doing certain things, because it gives labor all its meaning and the extra motivation you sometimes need on harder days.

The level of awareness mentioned above is more passive. It is the result of active work done in the background for years. Therefore, to be able to get there, you must adopt a proactive approach in the first place. This means that you will have to provoke your own mind, and trick yourself by questioning everything you do, see, hear, think and say.

Therefore, if in a discussion about race with your partner you feel uneasy or irritated, then before letting it out, stop and think. Ask yourself why you feel that way and if you would feel the same if the feedback was given by one of your white friends. If yes, why? Is it because you would feel less attacked on your whiteness?

A few tips I have found useful to do as a couple:

1. Recognize the Power Structure

To have a healthy relationship, both parties need to acknowledge the power dynamic in place. This makes me think about what Hector said to me once: 'Sometimes it is hard to see where the couple stops, and society begins.' I understand why someone would think that way, as if racism was something you could put in a box or demarcate. Unfortunately, it doesn't work like that. There will be no society without us and vice-versa; therefore, both are intertwined. Moreover, we, as individuals, tend to replicate in our micro-environment what we see out there on the bigger scale that is society. That's how you explain why, even within the LGBTQ+ community, you often find a hierarchy, and with hierarchy follows oppression. Even oppressed groups manage somehow to become the oppressor – I am thinking about gay people being transphobic or queer white people being racist and so forth.

In my past relationships, I have told my partner I will be open to discuss or answer any questions they may have with regards to race, and that I wouldn't be annoyed with them, as long as they were being mindful and honest in their approach. In return, I have asked them to also contribute to the talk about race. Why are Black people the only people expected to bring the subject up? For example, if there is a major news dropping like George Floyd's death, not mentioning it (obviously checking beforehand with your partner if it's the right moment to do so) feels like avoiding addressing the elephant in the room.

I think white people in interracial relationships should have full consciousness of their whiteness. Blackness exists in the context of whiteness; therefore, white folks do have to contribute to the discussion and take responsibility without taking too much space. It's about taking the right space at the right time, i.e. not taking emotional space in an argument related to race in order to defer the attention towards how they feel, vs how the Black person feels, when the Black person is the party who was hurt.

To conclude this sub-section, when I talk about the power dynamic, I am referring to privilege; hence this technique could be applied to any unbalanced protected characteristics that differ from one party to the other. For example, Hector and I had to deal with racial unbalance but also with gender unbalance, as they are non-binary and I am cis – at least for 99%.

2. Name It: 'We Are Talking About Race'

I have seen my partner feeling uneasy sometimes about saying the word *Black* as if it was a swearword, or about using the word *race* in an argument when they are clearly talking about it. I think not naming both is part of the problem. In fact, I believe it is shying away from normalizing the topic.

I have recently been listening to an amazing podcast called *Jins* about being Arab and/or Muslim and LGBTQIA+. I remember the presenter talking about how homophobic laws were brought in by settlers in Morocco. In fact, the law criminalizing homosexuality in Morocco (Article 489) was a replica of the exact same law that was implemented in France at the time. Ironically, in the French collective consciousness, Arabs and Muslim people are thought to discriminate against queer people more often, compared to their white French counterparts. It is hypocritical for French folks to now look like saviours and open-minded people, when they were the ones initiating prejudice in first place. The guest speaker Ludovic-Mohammed Zahed explains the above really well, and says that it is a subtle self-persuasion method where Arabs and/or Muslims start to believe themselves and what they'd been told, and became what everyone wanted them to be: homophobic.

I see some similarities with this phenomenon and the issues about race. In fact, if you charge the words *Black* and *race* with guilt or and discomfort, you are going to start feeling those emotions because you will have conditioned yourself to do so. Conversely, the more you name it, the more this feeling of uneasiness will go away, and it will feel natural to say it out loud. And technically, it's simpler to address an issue if we know what we are talking about, isn't it?

3. Tell Your Partner If They Are Not There Yet

White people are not made of sugar. I am not sure that makes much sense, so let me break it down to you.

What I mean is that we can often try to not say things as they are, in order to protect our partner, but in certain situations the truth must be told. It might be hard feedback for your white partner to hear, but it is a necessary step for them to grow.

In my situation, I had projected onto my partner, also based on our previous discussions, that they were somewhat *woke* enough to at least understand how white guilt works. But after months into the relationship, I realized that we were far away from a basic understanding of racism. As hard and uncomfortable it was for me to address it, I decided to do it. If they were as involved in this as they pretended to be, they would surely appreciate the feedback provided. So, after a huge argument about race that got unnecessarily escalated, I told them as it is: 'You are far behind; you must do better.'

If they thought they were high on the scale of allyship, I had to make them understand that they were lying to themself. As I mentioned before, the work must be done; it won't happen by itself and not overnight, so they had better start now. It will be hard to digest for them, but it's more about what your partner will do with this crucial piece information, now they are aware.

4. Accountability & Apology

Being accountable is a hard thing. It implies that you must accept that you messed up. In other words, it's acknowledging that you are human and that humans make mistakes. It's also acknowledging that because of a mistake of yours, even though unintentional, your partner has been hurt. If you made a mistake, white folks, just apologize genuinely. For me it does not mean only saying, 'I am sorry', it means knowing what you are sorry for. I will require you to self-analyse your conduct, and spot where it went all wrong, but also to see what you could have done better. That's when your apology is complete. Here is an example of apology: 'I am sorry for getting annoyed at you when you addressed my behaviour, which was clearly biased. I should not have been annoyed but instead, I should have listened actively. In the future I will… etc.' When that's done, you can just move on, unless your partner wants to discuss the matter further – for example, if it's not the first time a situation like this has happened. Anyway, as a ground rule it is not necessary to make the apology a massive thing; just make up for it. If you want to talk the talk, you better walk the walk! Actions speak louder!

5. Patience & Forgiveness

As a Black person, if you have chosen to listen to your heart and dated a white person, unless they have a PhD in racial injustice, you will have to be patient. As I've said before, the work can't be done overnight. Also, because white people are not Black, they won't be able to get it right all the time because they don't experience racism. So, you will have to be patient and to forgive sometimes, but not necessarily forget. However, there is a limit to the things you can take – unfortunately, only you know your level of tolerance. It will all depend on your emotional wellbeing and mental health. Do you have the emotional capacity right now? What are the things your relationship is bringing to your life that can balance out with the effort you are putting in?

I would say, though, that it's important to perhaps set up steps or a date when you will re-evaluate the progress your partner has made, and how you feel towards it. The important thing is that their learning process should not jeopardize your mental health. Speaking from experience, don't compartmentalize yourself; do not pretend it is not an issue. Don't only focus on things that are positive in the relationship if you see that your partner is not willing to putting the energy and the effort to educate themself. Loving someone does not give them a free pass to hurt you, or mean that you have to forget yourself.

To conclude, after reading all the above tips, try to put things in perspective by practicing. Indeed, communication, as you probably guessed, is a big part of the solution alongside the learning.

Communication Tips

Due to our language/cultural barrier, but also because both Hector and I are neurodivergent, we had to find ways to make sure we were communicating in the right way but also at the right time. Even more so when the subject discussed was loaded with intense emotions.

The below practice is a good way to check in with one another and to discuss any concerns, but also to celebrate each other. Because it can be an intense exercise, you should if possible link it to something positive: for example, order a takeaway at the end of the session, make some nice hot chocolate in order to reward yourself. It doesn't have to be food related; it could be a bath or anything that will make you both feel content and joyful.

Couple Exercise: Weekly Check-in

Frequency: This exercise can be done every week for a month. Then you and your partner can re-evaluate the frequency based on your needs, and perhaps increase the time between sessions. You can then choose to do monthly then bi-monthly catch-ups.

When: You need to both agree when exactly you are going to take time out. It must be a regular activity. I recommend it being the same day each week/month, and why not at the same time, when possible. This will allow both of you to prepare what you want to discuss in advance, but also to know that if you cannot address something in the moment, you still have an open window during the week to do so.

Goal: The aim of this exercise is to create a safe space where both parties can discuss important subject matters affecting the relationship, such as race. It's a time to allow yourself to be vulnerable, to ask questions, even complicated ones; moreover, it's a time to process. It will allow you to process confusing situations that have happened in the past days but with some distance, and with less strong emotions. It will help organize your thoughts and have easier conversations. It is a moment to get alignment and to work on a more organic way to communicate with one another. You will be able to track your progress and stagger the sessions, once you feel comfortable enough to bring things up in an effective and healthy manner between sessions.

Things to do before the catch up:

- **Get prepared**. Write down some questions you may have, and describe the emotions you felt regarding the situation(s) you want to address. Between discussions, write down things that may have triggered you in the past days or weeks, but also things that were positive. It's important to create a balance in the feedback to make it constructive.
- **Set up the rewards**. A treat to have once the check-in is complete. As I said before, because the exercise can be challenging, you should as much as possible link it to something positive. For example, treating yourself with a takeaway or your favourite homemade food. If you're aiming for the latter, perhaps cook it before the session so that you can enjoy it straight after. No matter what you

choose, it should be something you both like and that you would not usually go for. Definitely a positive outcome to look forward to!

During the meeting:

Both parties should have an equal amount of time to speak. No one should interrupt the other and the listening should be active. Hard thing to do when you've got ADHD.

So, if it is complicated to remember all the information at once for some of you, bring your notepad and write down the important points you'd like to cover as part of your answer.

At the end of the meeting:

Thank one another, just enjoy your treat and move on.

Interlude

Today I am sitting in a coffee place in Hove called Wolfox. I finished working less than an hour ago. I haven't written properly in weeks, because… life. I am working as a leader for a financial company and it is taking a lot of my time and energy. Despite Covid and because it's the end of the year, the activity is intense, which mean I have worked over 50 hours a week in the past three months – tough time. It doesn't leave much time to do the rest, and when the weekend comes, I am not willing to do anything that would require me to sit again in front of a screen for an extra hour or two. Hence most of the time, I just want to do nothing unless it's watching TV to numb my brain.

So unlike other days, today I finished earlier and decided to take this time to be productive and write. With the pandemic, there are not so many activities I can do and not so many places that are open. Therefore, leaving my flat to go out to a coffee place feels like a retreat. I am not joking: it's inspiring in a way because it's a change of scenery. Plus, I have nothing else to distract me… unless people watching counts?

Sitting here, I am wondering: why are we often so focused on ourselves that we cannot see what is in front of us? Sometimes things are obvious, just right here in front of our eyes, but we don't see, feel, hear or see them?

This whole interlude might seem out of context. Why am I suddenly talking about the meaning of the universe?

The response is straightforward because sitting at Wolfox and looking through the window, I realized that the barista had left to give the pastry leftovers to a homeless person across the street. And in a blink of an eye, it just took me back to the moment, and I grounded myself – for an instant, I wasn't the centre of the universe. I was there and so were these people, also breathing the same air, at the same time. I found the gesture of the barista thoughtful; we often forget that people can also be nice nowadays. So, I am just embracing this kind reminder.

CHAPTER 2

Breaking Up & Processing

So here we are. I am writing this chapter while I am sitting at the hairdresser. I took the decision to cut it all – my hair, I mean. I am a strong believer in haircut therapy. I think that hair accumulates our stress and keeps memories. For a year and a half, I have let my hair grow, then turned it into dreadlocks and finally added extensions to some of my baby locks. So today I am rebirthing, I am starting fresh, I am cutting out the fringe and the rest. I shaving my head and I am dying it pink.

Interestingly, my hairdresser is planning on moving out of Brighton in January. I am feeling odd about it because first, he is someone that I really like, but also because if you are a Black person, you must know the struggle of finding a good hairdresser. Someone who you can trust enough to not damage your hair, to take care of it properly, because afro hair care is not the same as 'European' hair care.

Jack my hairdresser (name changed to keep anonymity) and I have history; we had sex after my breakup with Camille over three years ago. I was lost, sad and I wanted to test myself, I guess.

Camille and I dated for two years. I wanted to marry her. As a matter of fact, probably a month before she broke up with me, I started revealing to a few close friends about my plan to propose. Life decided otherwise, though. While I thought that the breakup took away all the chances I had to spend the rest of my life with her, I was wrong, because despite the breakup she stayed around. We became friends – as surprising this was for me, as I tend not to stay close with my exes. With her it seemed the right thing to do; it was organic. She is one of the people who knows me best.

You must wonder why we broke up, which is a fair question, so let me explain it to you. After a strong disagreement, Camille decided to end our relationship. No, I must be honest here too, so let me tell you what really happened. Rewind.

After a strong disagreement, I decided to end things with Camille. At the time, she was not aligned with my decision to break up, and she wanted us to try again. I decided to sleep on the couch that night; in the morning, I told her that I had changed my mind – however, she had too. While I wanted to give us another chance, she was, to the contrary, determined to end things between us, and nothing I could have said at that time would have made her review her decision.

Doesn't it remind you of another situation? Perhaps something similar but more recent? Yes, it is similar in some ways to what I am going through with Hector currently. But why are we repeating patterns? Why can't we learn from our previous mistakes?

With Hector I am torn between the desire to go back with them but also with the realization that there is something dysfunctional between us. Not being with Hector has made me realize that I need some time for myself to grieve my previous relationship with Julie but also to find myself again. I want to reconnect with them but I have come to the conclusion that I could benefit from some alone time in order to process things. Nonetheless, I am supposed to meet them over the weekend. If we are deciding to get back together, it would have to be gradually because I cannot do a full-on relationship with anyone else right now but myself. Moreover, since we have now spent almost a week apart, I am starting to understand what my needs are.

So, here is a non-exhaustive list of my needs as a Black queer woman. Perhaps they can help you understand yours too:

1. To have my feelings considered by my partner.

I have often been questioned regarding the validity of my feelings, especially when they are negative feelings such as anger or unhappiness. As Black women, we should be allowed to say it as it is, without fearing being stereotyped as an angry Black woman. We should allow ourselves to be angry, because angriness is a feeling that white people are allowed to feel, so why can't we?

2. To feel desired by my partner.

This is a hard one, because if feelings are down to each one of us individually, there must be some consensus on what desire means and how it will be displayed in the relationship. Because of anti-Blackness we, Black people, can sometimes feel inferior compared to our white counterparts, who are broadly considered to be models of beauty and intelligence. Speaking for myself, I have sometimes, throughout my childhood and adult life, felt like I was a fraud, not pretty enough, or just average. I am clearly aware that the internal struggle of feeling unattractive can both affect white and black folks. However, it is important to emphasize the fact that if white folks are feeling ugly or unpretty, this is never related to the color of their skin. Unlike white folks, Black folks are competing against unrealistic beauty expectations. In fact, although skin shade is one of the criteria of universal beauty standards, there is more to it: 'valuing whiteness as beauty comes down to more than just skin color. It's also about the Anglicized features[1] we associate with white women: smaller noses, thinner lips, less prominent curves'[2] wrote Maisha Z. Johnson. Maisha's article mentioned the Doll Test, which I believe is a good, even though quite disturbing, tool to concretely understand beauty standards on a much deeper level. For those who haven't watched this video, the Doll Test is an experiment initially led in the 40s by two African American psychologists Mamie and Kenneth Clark. The aim was to study the impact of psychological effects of segregation on African American children. In this video, you see Black children facing two dolls, one white and the other Black. They are then being asked

---

1 Eurocentric Beauty Standards: A Global Disease – Gabriella Tranchina. germmagazine.com.

2 10 Ways The Beauty Industry Tells You Being Beautiful Means Being White – Maisha Z. Johnson. Everyday Feminism – thebodyisnotanapology.com

binary questions, such as 'Which doll is ugly/pretty?' 'Which doll is nice/mean?' etc. Almost all the children, who are Black themselves, associate anything related to being bad and unbeautiful to the Black doll, and conversely all good and beautiful traits to the white doll. When they are asked why they choose the white doll to be the nicest, they straightaway mention the doll's skin color: 'Because she is white' but also refer to the Anglicized features: 'Because she has blue eyes'. Even though this study was initially led on African American children, the findings apply to almost all Black children, despite their geographical location. In fact, this experiment was then repeated and revisited several times in the 90s and in 2000, but also in different countries, and the results remained the same. The impact racism has on Black people is undeniable and universal.

Watching this video, you understand the damage anti-Blackness has perniciously inflicted upon Black people's sense of self. So, before reading this chapter, perhaps you thought that you were being too needy when you asked your partner to show the desire they have towards you?

I can assure you that you are not! It is NOT a big ask and it is NOT coming from nowhere. You, I, we deserve it!

I just want to clarify: when I am talking about desire, I am not referring specifically to sex. I mean being pro-actively showing gratitude, complimenting, closeness in terms of both intimacy and/or sex.

To conclude, because of the racial unbalance in interracial relationships, white partners should be showing a higher appreciation, compared to what they show when they are dating white folks. Speaking for myself, I'd say that being worshipped by my partner is comforting, especially on days when I have lower self-esteem. It reinforces the message I am finding hard to tell myself everyday, which is as follows: *I do not have to be white to be desired and worshipped – I am enough as I am: Black, worthy and beautiful.*

If I must draw a parallel to my relationship with Hector, I'd say that I never had to actively think about this need before I dated them. The reason being that I used to date people who were highly demonstrative in terms of displays of affection. However, Hector is not like that. They are struggling to express their emotions in general, so I started to question myself. It did not happen overnight, and I did not realize straight away that this was an issue; it had to materialize through something else… jealousy. I started to feel insecure when they would spend time with their exes who were, as you can imagine, all white. I was comparing myself to them but always leading to the conclusion that I was maybe not enough. Hector had, in the past, been saying that I was gorgeous and intelligent, but I refused to listen. While in my relationship with Julie or other exes, they were amazed by my person, but with Hector I had the impression they loved me and found me attractive, but that was it. I recognized that the way they were showing me attention was not enough. I needed more, I needed to feel special. Is that a big ask? We've already answered that, haven't we!

While there is an undeniable responsibility for the white queer person to make their Black queer partner feel desired, I realized by breaking up with Hector that both partners also have to meet halfway.

As Black people, we must unlearn societal constructs and perceived ideas of beauty. We must identify our internalized anti-Blackness, and tackle it to then be able to embrace ourselves. Of course, let's be honest, it makes things easier if your partner is supporting you along the way, but we must do it for ourselves and not so much for the person we are with. We have to heal our transgenerational trauma – aka legacy of slavery and colonization,[3] commonly referred to nowadays simply as *systemic racism.* We have to daily celebrate our melanin, daily say that we are beautiful, and that we are smart and powerful. If you don't feel it yet, that's fine; carry on. Fake it until you make it. First and foremost, we have to recognize that despite what the media or society is forcing us to believe, WE ARE ENOUGH!

We are going to pause here, and take a break – a poetry break, in fact. As a Black/PoC reader, it may be a lot to digest, as you are probably able to relate and if you are a white reader, it is still a lot to process. So let's take some time off. I have written a poem called *You Are Enough* and I feel like it will fit in perfectly with what we just talked about. So if you can, go make

---

3 The roots of European racism lie in the slave trade, colonialism – and Edward Long. David Olusoga. The Guardian.

yourself a tea or a coffee, take some water or any drink you fancy. Nothing can also be an option. Sit comfortably and breathe in, hold it for four seconds and breathe out; it is time to relax. I call it a break for a reason, so make the most of it.

YOU ARE ENOUGH

Earlier today I wanted to cry

Cry because I was hurt deep inside

People usually think that I am pretty

Some folks even say that I am beautiful, but is that it?

But then they don't wanna know about me further

Sometime they don't really wanna dig deeper

I am conscious of who I am, I can be passionate

That not something that I hide, I am like that, I am honest

I try hard you know to moderate myself

But, I cannot, from a day to another, change and be someone else.

I wanted to write a sad poem initially

Then I changed my mind, I am who I am and unapologetic.

If you actually take the time to go through all those layers,

You will see that even if I am strong, I've been hurt.

29 years of love, loss, and grief.

29 years when I had to build myself in order to be me.

I had to be proud of myself otherwise no one will,

I had to be strong and say you are enough Méfi

I am someone who cares a lot for others

Maybe because I hope one day someone will care for me that much?

I intended to write something full of sadness

But, while writing I realised it doesn't have to be that way.

Because life is made of moments when we get hurt, moments of doubt,

Words that people can say that really impact.

I initially allowed myself to go through this sadness,

And I came from it stronger, with more lightness.

I am at a moment in my life when I try to see things as positive as they can be,

It can be challenging, sometimes hard to deal with.

But I try as much as I can to push myself higher,

I know what I am like, and when I deserve better.

At the end of the day if people cannot see who I am then, that's their loss

Because after all those years of struggle I can say, that I am enough

Next on the non-exhaustive list of needs:

3. To communicate clearly and frequently.

This one is highly affected by culture. In fact, I have lived in France almost all my life so when I moved here, I realized the way I was taught about how to communicate was somehow drastically different from my British counterparts. Indeed, French people are seen as rude because we say things as they are, with no sugar coating. If we don't like someone, we won't try to be nice, but when we are affectionate, it's real; we don't have time for 'faux-semblants' and we don't pretend unless it's work related, and still…

Something I have noticed since I moved to the UK over six years ago was this British politeness. I must say English people got me initially, with their fake-friendliness and this pretence that everything is well. It took me a few months and several discussions with foreigners who verbalized the same experience to understand. While now I know the trick, I still managed to be fooled from time to time. For example, in the supermarket, when I answer, 'Good, and you?' to the question 'How are you doing?' from cashiers who literally do not give a damn about my answer and therefore, nine times out of ten, never answer me back. I often feel silly, but I have got used to it, I guess. Sometimes, I ask myself, though: *Méfi, haven't you learned anything after living here for six years?*

If not communicating effectively with cashiers does not have much impact in my life, I must admit that it has become an issue with partners. Imagine having to navigate your emotions plus having to express them in a language that is not your mother tongue.

And besides the language itself, you also have to manage the cultural aspects – such as British politeness. The issue with British politeness is that often people tend not to say what they really think, not to hurt someone or to create an awkward situation. I have always asked Hector to tell me what they really think; if they disagree about something I don't want them to say 'Yes' if they think otherwise. I value honesty and authenticity, but I also want them to feel like they can tell me how they really feel.

Because fake politeness is really ingrained in British culture, I had to train myself in order to spot realness vs fakeness. When I ask Hector about something and they say, 'Yes it's fine', sometimes I am not sure they are being real or polite. So now, when I get a doubt, I ask them, 'Are you trying to British me?' which suddenly makes the awkwardness go away. I have created that saying/verb because I think it perfectly suits those kinds of situations. It is short and straightforward. It can also be used as an order: 'Don't British me.' Since then, we have both used this saying between us.

I remember one day Hector asking for advice. They wanted to know if they should contact one of their exes. I did not see why not, considering she contributed to Hector's 30th birthday present despite them not talking to one another anymore. I said to Hector that if she did not want to be friends with them anymore, she probably wouldn't have contributed to their birthday gift – at least that's what I would do. Hector nicely made me realize that I had probably been once again 'Britishized', and that their ex was just being polite.

I am wondering how native British folks do it. How do you know when you have been 'Britishized'? I myself find it hard and confusing to decode the British politeness: 'Indeed, communicating with a British person entails having the ability to understand not only what is explicitly stated, but also what is implied.'[4] wrote Iweta Kalinowska

I admire this ability. I am not quite there yet, even after almost seven years, but I am getting better.

4. To be allowed to let the guard down and be sad.

It often feels like in the relationship, when the other person is down, then it is our role to lead and keep our pain in the closet. To pretend we don't need to be cared for, that we can handle it all. While sometimes the situation forces us to behave that

---

4 The truth behind British (im)politeness – Iweta Kalinowska. termcoord.eu.

way, I believe that we also put a lot of pressure on ourselves to be the carer. Not because we want to, but because we have been taught to do so. There are no other behaviours we are thinking of adopting instead, because as Black folks, we are told to put ourselves second, to be selfless.

In order to fight our anti-Blackness inner voices, we must be careful and sometime analyse our conduct and motivations. Obviously, I am not asking you to care less for your partner but just not to lose yourself on the way. Because damn, you also deserve to be cared for!

In my situation, I have put Hector's feelings above mine several times, because they have been more vocal about their depression. Therefore, I tend to close down and not share how I feel, even when I am feeling down. I often wish they could understand how I feel without me saying anything, but the truth is that Hector is no mind-reader. I naturally struggle to open up because I fear being vulnerable. Hence, when I have someone in front of me who is already heavily down, I innately go back into my shell and wait until my feelings eventually get better. In my situation, this is the result of years of struggle following my mother's death. When she passed away, I was nineteen years old. I was angry against the world because it was unfair, and especially to friends and acquaintances who still had their mum, even though they had nothing to do with my mother's death. One day, I remember I was on a train back home from nursing school. It was less than a year after she passed away. I was on the train with three friends, and they started talking about their parents, asking each other what their parents did for a living and so on. I was angry and hurt since I felt like they were being insensitive, so I said to them, 'At least you still have a mother.' It wasn't the first time I had said something passive aggressive during similar conversations. However, while before, they used to not say anything back, that time one of them unexpectedly replied: 'Yes we know it's hard, but you will have to stop saying this all the time.' At that moment, I realized that despite whatever I could say and however angry I could be, it would not change a thing, as no one would be able to understand what I was going through. At that moment, I decided not to say anything anymore and just suck it up – no more comments. What was the point anyway? From that moment and for all moments that came after that one, I wore armor to protect myself. What that friend said on that day is forever engraved in my mind.

I went off track a bit, but to go back on topic, Black people – but actually no one – should put their mental health at stake to please someone else. Black minds matter as much as white minds do.

Interlude

First Coming Out Stories

I remember this teenage lover; his name was Léo. I recall being jealous of one of his friends, Emma, who he was spending a lot of time with. I recall Léo telling me not to worry because she was probably gay. I remember pausing when he said that, not really knowing how to process the information. Sure, I guess I did not have to worry then. While I was not worried anymore about them two getting together, I recall being intrigued by this new information regarding Emma's sexuality. At that time, I'd already had couple of queer experiences. I had my first kiss with a girl at fourteen; her name was Lena. We met in summer camp in Andorra, and she was pretty. I did not know I was attracted to her until we kissed. I attended a performing arts camp, so the main activities were music, dance, visual arts, and theatre. The aim of this camp was to create a theatrical play that we would perform live for the locals at the end of the stay. You can imagine the pressure, especially when you are fourteen.

One cool thing was that every other day, we would have an open-mic night; we could sign up and perform anything we'd like. Lena and I attended few open-mic nights but that evening, Noah, her boyfriend at the time, was performing. I can't remember what he was doing exactly but he was there on stage while Lena and I were sitting next to each other as part of the audience. She seemed sad but I did not know why. She lay her head on my shoulder, I started to run my fingers through her hair, and we hugged. We were facing each other; her lips were now so close that in a blink of an eye without thinking, I kissed her. It felt like the right thing to do in that moment, but by the look she gave me, I understood that she was not expecting that at all. She seemed confused; I did not know what else to say except to say I was sorry. Sorry for not asking, sorry because some people probably saw us kiss, as it was pretty crowded in the basement that night. Even though Noah was there, he did not witness what happened. Lena told him after, though, because she could not hide anything from him. They had a deep connection; I think she loved him. The end of the summer camp unofficially marked the end of their relationship. They kept in touch after the camp; unfortunately, Noah ended their love story for good a couple of months after, because it turned out he was gay.

Lena was my first queer romance. We exchanged a few letters after the summer camp ended. I remember waiting days, weeks and sometimes months could pass before I received one of her letters. I was wondering what she was doing, because we did not have mobile phones back then. I read one of her letters to my mother once – not all of it, of course. I knew for a fact that a few lines would have shocked her because Lena and I used to talk to each other quite openly.

So, this correspondence with Lena lasted for six months, perhaps more, until it died one day. I had to wait a couple of months before I received a response to my last letter. I remember losing faith, thinking that maybe she had stopped loving me; maybe she had met someone. The only sure thing I knew was that I did not know a thing.

In her last letter, she explained that her dad had found our correspondence letters and that he wanted her out of the house. She was saying goodbye and ending our relationship because she did not have any other option, I guess.

I still have some of Lena's letters somewhere; I might read some of them tomorrow. This story is over seventeen years old, but I remember it as if it happened yesterday. It's weird how our brain works sometimes; it has a selective memory.

Following this epistolary romance with Lena, I had another queer experience when I was sixteen. It was just before Léo, actually. Her name was Adalia; she was a German exchange student. Before I carry on telling you more about this Franco-Germanic romance, I must reveal a crucial detail. For some reasons that I won't mention here, I spent my last year of college in boarding school – that's all you need to know for now. Back to the story. It was summertime, 7pm-ish, and we were all having dinner, when I left the table because it was too hard to see Benjamin, the guy I liked, getting closer to Pauline, my roommate. I went to sit outside at the canteen entrance to smoke a cigarette when Adalia came to join me.

Seeing that I was crying, she put her arm around me. She tried to comfort me, saying that if she were Benjamin, she would have chosen me. It made me smile. I thought she was nice particularly because we did not really know each other – we had probably only spoken twice before then. Nevertheless, Adalia opened her arms wider and pulled me towards her to give me a hug. It felt comforting. However, when I moved myself back, she then kissed me. Even though I was surprised, I did not stop her. In fact, I told her to go somewhere safer and hidden, so we could carry on kissing. Kids!

Adalia and my romance did not last. The main reason was that she wanted to go official and be out at school, but I couldn't do it. My cousin was also in our school and I wasn't ready to come out to her. At that time, I felt like Adalia was being selfish. She wanted to be out, but she would then leave France at the end of the year to go back to Germany, as if nothing had happened. It would then be easier for her to pretend that this whole romance had never existed; still I would have to carry this burden for good. What would my cousin think of me? Would she have to be bullied because of me? I couldn't do this to her or to myself, so I politely declined Adalia's offer. She was disappointed but okay with it, and so was I.

Nevertheless, because we were dating, I did come out to two of my closest boarding school friends. They happened to be really chilled about it. It was refreshing because Adalia and I could hold hands and kiss when we were hanging out with them both, as if there were no big deal.

How odd is that story? How did Adalia know I would not freak out when she kissed me, especially when she knew I was crying for a boy? Did she have what we call the gaydar/queerdar? Anyway, I never heard back from Adalia once she left France for Germany. I tried to look for her on social media years later, in 2008 when Facebook was launched in France, but vainly. The cheeky side of this story: because we were both at boarding school and because our rooms were literally next to one another, we used to sneak in each other's bed to *play*… no explanation needed.

Anyway, I did come out to my cousin in the end, but it was years and years later, once I had moved to Brighton. That's how long it takes to come out sometimes. As a reminder, coming out is not one of the requirements in order to belong to the queer community.

In the past days, I have felt highly melancholic. Perhaps because it's the end of the year. Let's say also that lockdown doesn't help, when you are stuck at home there is not so much you can do. Nonetheless, this period is for me one of the strangest and saddest, as we are getting closer to December, which is when my mother passed away: 26th December 2008. Time flies, and most of the good memories fade away to only leave you with the pain, which unfortunately lasts forever. People say grief gets easier with time. I am not sure it gets easier, I think we just learn to live with it, that's all. I usually reminisce about the past closer to the end of the year, wondering what has become of the ones I once loved. Are they alive and happy? Do they sometimes remember me?

I am going to share with you one of my first pieces of writing, from when I was seventeen. It's an extract from what was called *La gazette tome II*. I found this autobiographical novel on my old iMac; I thought I would share some of it with you. This text is about my mum. I actually wrote it when she was still alive; it was part of a paragraph about Valentine's Day, where I decided to talk about my loved ones. I am voluntarily keeping the original extract in French for those of you who happen to speak French. I have translated it below for the non-French-speaking readers. I have tried my best to make it rhyme, as that is the case in the French version. Be kind and not too judgmental while reading this poem – I was only a teenager when I wrote it!

En Francais

Et oui même si je n'en parle pas souvent,

Dans mon cœur elle est quotidiennement.

Vous vous demandez de qui je peux bien parler.

On va dire que c'est la première fois que je vais en parler longuement en vérité.

Même si je suis loin de toi,

Mon corps est ici mais mon esprit avec toi.

Il ne se passe pas un jour sans que je ne pense à toi de tout mon être,

Je n'ose pas souvent te le dire, mais je t'aime en fait.

Et oui, vous ne le saviez peut-être pas,

Mais je suis amoureuse d'une femme plus vieille que moi.

Une femme au passé et au futur extraordinaire,

Une femme simple qui est ma mère.

Une femme belle et gentille,

Qui a su je crois me pardonner pas mal de bêtises.

Même si parfois j'aurais aimé ne pas faire partie de ce monde, ni du suivant,

J'aurais regretté de ne pas t'avoir comme maman.

Je pense que c'est une des premières et dernières fois, qu'ainsi je parlerai de toi.

Non pas que j'ai honte de toi, mais plutôt de moi.

D'avoir osé au fond te faire souffrir,

D'avoir osé par moment être la pire des filles.

De t'avoir laissé et faite pleurer,

De te réprimander à chaque faux pas qui est en fait bien fait.

Si parfois il m'arrive de te prendre la tête pour des broutilles,

C'est pas peur qu'avec la distance tu ne m'oublies.

Mais en vérité d'être loin de toi c'est ce qui me fait le plus mal, de ne plus te voir au quotidien,

De rigoler avec toi me faisait du bien.

Car en vérité sans toi je suis perdue, mais je n'ose pas te le dire pour que tu sois triste et à ton tour perdue.

In English

Even though I am not talking about her often as I should,

She is forever in my mind and in everything I do.

You must be confused and wonder who I am talking about.

Let's say it's the first time I am going to share, so let me unpack.

Even though I am not here with you, even though I am far away,

I will always be here for you, in every step of the way.

No days are passing by without me thinking of you,

I am never telling you this enough, but I love you.

I have not told you so you may not be aware,

But I am in love with a woman who is a bit older.

A woman with a bright future and an extraordinary past,

An easy-going woman who is my mother in fact.

She is beautiful and a kind woman,

Who loves me despite my mistakes that she has forgiven.

Even though I sometimes feel I don't belong here,

You make me feel that I am wrong and that I deserve to live.

It's the first and last time I will talk about you that way.

Because being vulnerable makes me feel uncomfortable and ashamed.

How did I dare make you suffer, I wasn't an easy child,

I have argued with you often even when you were right.

If I annoy you sometimes with unnecessary stuff,

It's because I fear that with the distance you will forget about us.

But the truth is that being away from you is making me suffer the most,

Cause being around you, laughing with you made me feel I was enough.

But I won't tell all of that, even if it's the truth,

Cause I know you will feel sad, and that it will hurt you.

Thinking about my first coming out story, I outed myself to my first real boyfriend, Frank, back in college when I was fifteen. He was so chilled about it, and he never questioned me; it all felt natural to him. Frank broke up with me after six months of being together – I remember he was my rock at the time especially when my mother got diagnosed with breast cancer.

A year later, after we broke up, he confessed to me that he never dated other girls after me. He said he couldn't feel anything with girls, not romantic feelings, but that with me it was different. Frank did not know it at the time, but he was gay. He came out to me maybe a year later after that discussion. It was not a big surprise, if I am being honest. His admiration for Britney, Christina Aguilera, and J-Lo, joined with the fact that he was effeminate, did raise my suspicions, although I was not about to jump to conclusions only based on clichés.

When I think about my queerness, I think about all of this. I think about the past heteronormative romance and love stories that contributed to my queerness. As you may have noticed, some of the relationships I had, with Frank, for example, were relationships involving two queer people who ignored the fact that they were queer at the time. So even though it was perceived back then as a straight romance, it was not the case. In fact, it's not so much about who you date but more about who you are and how you identify. In other words, who you date does not define who you are. Even if I know you know this already, it is always nice to remind ourselves from time to time. Nevertheless, knowing the above won't protect you from people perceiving you or your relationship in a way that is different from how you see it yourself. That's why this reminder is necessary every so often. It's an empowering statement, emphasizing that we are queer enough. There is no one-size-fits-all approach. There is not only one way to be: we are all unique individuals with similar identities creating different narratives.

CHAPTER 3

Mental Health & Self-care

While others may be contributing to our own process of self-love, we must be the highest contributor. I cannot lie; I do appreciate it when someone I don't know compliments me for what I am wearing or just for who I am. While I did not realize the impact this had on my mental health and self-esteem, going through a pandemic made me realize sooner than expected that I was taking it for granted. When I talk about compliments, I mean micro-validation and appreciation comments such as 'You look great today', 'It's good to see you', 'I love your outfit' etc. The above comments did make me feel seen. Covid has forced us to imagine a new way of life, a different way to interact with others. Since last year, I have been working only from home, managing a team of seventeen-plus colleagues from the 'comfort' of my living room. My back has been struggling with the adjustment, since we had no budget from my company to invest in our workstations.

I must admit it has been challenging to maintain my sanity and a healthy work-life balance. Don't get me wrong, working from home has its benefits: like now, I have time for lunch and I am often taking the full hour I am entitled to. At the office, this would barely happen, and I would usually eat at my desk and just get on with it or I would grab something at the canteen, sit in the kitchen and eat my food in less than 30 minutes. So, this is a significant improvement that must be acknowledged, and for which I am grateful.

On the other hand, your home environment is both your office and your playground. If you have a large flat or house, it's hard but manageable, but if you live in a studio or house share like almost all my team, it can easily become a mess. Being physically in the office 24/7 means that when it's legally time to finish work, you often stay. Because why not, right? Especially during lockdown, it's easy to say to yourself, 'I am just answering a last email', or 'It's not as if I had something else exciting to do instead'. Then it is few hours later and you realize that you are still sitting at your desk, still working. A never-ending cycle.

Moreover, I believe that employees working from home are expected to always work, no matter their physical or mental health situation. Because they are already at home, nothing should theoretically prevent them from opening their laptop, right?

So, there is this kind of untold and pressuring consensus that you must carry on working at the same pre-Covid standards, despite the circumstances. Nevertheless, my company provided great mental health support throughout the year. Indeed, we have access to free counsellors available 24/7 by call and a mental health hub, which is pretty cool, considering. I believe there is still more awareness to raise about mental health, though, on an individual level. Because even if a company provides some great tools, it's ultimately down to the individuals to feel like they can and should use them. Hence, since the pandemic, I have been vocal about the support available within the company. I have made sure my team knows where they can access it. I have also been transparent about my mental health and shared one of my struggles with them.

In fact, last year, a few months after the first national lockdown, I had a massive breakdown. The uprising of the Black Lives Matter movement did really affect me. I started dissociating – something that I never had done before. This sensation of being both here and absent in one single moment. I think that also the breakup with Julie triggered it.

While I wasn't able to see it at the time, I now understand that all the events following George Floyd's death played a role in my breakup with Julie. To some extent, obviously. I think it made me realize that I was not my full self in that relationship, and that I was putting my Blackness aside. Not fully embracing both my Black and queer identity, just to make her feel comfortable. Julie had a serious lack of knowledge of both subjects, combined with an unwillingness to learn. After an argument about race, she would cry and say that she would do better, that she would one day be this woke person… blah blah blah bull***. It took me a while to recognize she was just lying to me, and that she wasn't ready to put in the required amount of energy to fill the gap. She did read a few books on these topics, but she did not understand the content because the motivation for learning was not genuine. She was doing it just for the sake of it, but not in order to become a better person. So obviously the effort never lasted, and she could not understand how she might use the resources she'd learned and apply them to our relationship.

ME and ADHD

I was recently diagnosed with ADHD –attention deficit hyperactivity disorder. I am still trying to get my head around this, to be honest, trying to understand but first and foremost to accept it. With the pandemic but especially the lockdown, I have really struggled to regulate my emotions, but not only that. If you had asked me a few months before what ADHD was, I would have told you that it was something affecting white boys. The image I had in my head was unmanageable white kids screaming and running everywhere.

While reading the symptoms, I realized this stereotype was far from true. Not only was ADHD not a white person condition only, but also it manifests itself in different forms, including a non-hyperactive form called inattentiveness. In fact, there are three types:

- *Inattentive type, known as ADD (attention deficit disorder).* This form includes symptoms such as forgetfulness, being distracted easily, appearing withdrawn, disorganization, lack of focus.
- *Hyperactive-impulsiveness type, known as ADHD.* Symptoms associated: experiencing on-the-go feelings, fidgeting when seated, interrupting people when they speak, constant thinking looping/overthinking.

- *Combination type, ADHD/ADD.* With a variety of symptoms from the above types. This is the form I am affected by.

Despite being a developmental condition, which means 'symptoms [and] behaviours are due to the brain developing differently in key stages of development'[5], this condition is not taken seriously compared to some others. ADHD has a severe stigma attached to it and behaviour issues are seen as intentional, controllable tantrums and laziness. There is a shared disbelief that ADHD is neither a medical condition nor a disability.

I have been struggling a lot lately, without realizing I have actually been struggling all my life. Being aware of this diagnosis made me understand that many behaviours I have are not as 'normal' as I thought they were. I understand that not everyone feels the same, although when I thought I had a problem with rejection and emotional regulation, it was true. It was not something I had imagined. During my young years, I was hypersensitive; I remember my sister saying that I was crying too much for nothing. In primary school, my teacher referred me to a speech therapist as I was not talking at all in class. After an evaluation, it was established that I had no speech impairments – I was just really silent and withdrawn.

---

5 Neurodiversity and other conditions https://adhdaware.org.uk/what-is-adhd/neurodiversity-and-other-conditions/#:~:text=ADHD%20is%20a%20neurodevelopmental%20condition,as%20a%20very%20young%20child.

In my teen years, I used to have extremely volatile emotions, both up and down. I recall cutting my wrist several times after one of my sisters said I was fat and useless. I wasn't able to channel my anger and sadness. The intensity of my emotions did affect several, if not all, of my romantic relationships, and most recently the one with Camille. At the time I did not understand why I was often frustrated with her. Getting my diagnosis helped me realize that in most situations, I was frustrated with her because I was feeling overwhelmed. In fact, when that happens, I tend to involuntarily unload my frustration on myself but also on people who are around me, especially my partners. Overwhelming situations happen all the time: for me, multitasking can easily turn into an overwhelming situation, because I must do several things at once and it's too much for my brain to organize and manage.

Funnily enough, before I knew I had ADHD, I used to use that word to describe how I felt in some situations. I also had a note on my computer saying, 'Listen actively, no interruption' – and this is without realizing how much it resonated with my eventual diagnosis.

Currently, I am struggling the most with the non-stop thinking, and the emotional dysregulation.

Being diagnosed has affected me in unexpected ways. While I have been doubting myself more, I have also found a community of ADHDers. So many people have ADHD/ADD, and so many people are experiencing similar things like I do. I am – we are – not alone. It's actually a solace to know that.

For folks who have been diagnosed recently, I would recommend joining a virtual group to connect with other ADHDers. No need to interact directly if you are a shy person, but you can just read the comments. It does help sometimes. In terms of Facebook groups, I would recommend 'Adult ADHD/ADD Support & Chat Hub' or 'ADHD Diagnosed in Adulthood'.

More often, groups are global, and people join from all around the world – that's the case for the groups above.

I have been trying to educate myself more about ADHD, and one of the easiest ways I've found is to listen to podcasts while I cook. One of my favourite is called *I Have ADHD*, hosted by Kristen Carder. Because she also has ADHD, it makes the content more accurate and relatable. I often use Instagram when I am looking for ADHD content. It is usually easy information to digest. In terms of resources made by Black and Brown folks for Black and Brown folks, you can follow *The Black Spectrum* and also *ADHD Babes* on Instagram; both are UK-based communities. I think it's important to have resources made by Black folks in particular, to break the stigma. Black and white people are equally affected by ADHD. However, due to systemic racism, Black folks are less likely to get diagnosed. This is due to both anti-Blackness stereotypes but also financial inequality between races.

Taking myself as an example, getting a diagnosis cost me £380. This is the price for a one-hour assessment with a private psychiatrist and does not include the prescription of a treatment. I could have gotten a referral from my GP and planned to have a consultation via the NHS, but my GP told me the waiting list was long even if I was to exercise my *right to choose*. Delays are apparently even more important due to the pandemic. 'If you are registered with a GP surgery in England and you are referred by a GP to a consultant or specialist in mental health, you have the legal right to choose the organization (qualified provider) to whom you are referred, as long as that organization is providing that service in another part of England[6].'

Even though the consultation was expensive, I had the privilege to afford it. Saying this does not diminish how tough my current job is, and how I much I deserve this money – it's just a fact.

Anyway, while it was quick to get the appointment for the ADHD assessment, it took the practice over two weeks to email me the report. Once I received the report, I got referred to the NHS. Otherwise, I would have had to pay an extra £300 on top of the initial consultation in order to get prescribed medication. If I had booked both consultations at the same time, I would have gotten a £85 discount and paid £595 instead of £680 – bargain! I still struggle to understand how mental health care is considered a luxury – clearly for that price, it is not accessible to all. To reduce the cost, I decided to only go for the assessment. Once I got the diagnosis, I realized that

---

6 https://www.nhs.uk/Services/Trusts/Overview/DefaultView.aspx?id=145405

perhaps I would have also benefited from having medication. However, when I called, I was told the above, so no way I was going to pay that extra money, not now. I had expenses for my car coming in at over £200, a year's worth of a water bill to pay (that's another story) which was over £400, and then soon my electricity bill increased, based on my usage of heating over the winter.

Thankfully, apparently if you have a diagnosis of ADHD, and if your GP is comfortable enough, then they can initiate it. Luckily, like mine, your GP surgery might also have psychiatric practitioners, making it easier for you to get adequate treatment. Nevertheless, I contacted my GP with the diagnosis letter over two weeks ago, and nothing has happened yet. This process has now been on-going for a month and a half. It is indeed not too bad compared to the six months to a year minimum waiting time, but still.

The ADHD assessment itself was something else. At first, I had to complete several questionnaires. One of them had to be completed by my partner and another one by my parents – a bit intrusive, isn't it? I then emailed back the answers to the secretary. On the day of the assessment, I received a video call from the psychiatrist, a white man perhaps in his late fifties. He was smiling a lot, almost as if he was not taking what I was saying seriously. He asked me similar questions to those I had already answered in the initial questionnaires, to then come to the conclusion that I had *mild* ADHD. He insisted on the *mild* aspect. Because I have been able to maintain my job, and to do things like hang out with my friends (pre-Covid), then ADHD therefore did not have too much impact on my life, he said. People who have *severe* ADHD, he continued, cannot work or have a social life. I was surprised by this conclusion because first, yes, I have maintained my job, but I had to put coping mechanisms in place. It wasn't all easy-peasy. Furthermore, with the current working-from-home environment and Covid-related stress, my ADHD symptoms had got worse. My anxiety level has been through the roof, leading me to a serious mental breakdown last year with symptoms such as dissociation. Moreover, even though I have maintained my role within my company, I have been switching jobs every two/two and half years. Mostly because after some time, I get bored of the lack of challenge or lose my interest unless I am really passionate about what I do. Nonetheless, I am still delivering – even overachieving – at work most of the time. Anyway, I have learned with time to recognize the signs, so I often start looking for a new job when that feeling of boredom arises.

Getting the term *mild* added to my ADHD diagnosis was kind of invalidating my experience as an ADHDer. In fact, when I shared my feelings on social media about the '*mild* ADHD diagnosis', numerous people told me that adding a level of severity to a neurodivergent diagnosis was outdated. In fact, beyond similarities there can be between ADHDers, there is not only one way to have ADHD.

I remember how I felt when the psychiatrist turned his cameras on. Even though his whiteness was something I expected, I still had a tiny hope that he would be Black. Trying to cover my disappointment but also the fear of being misdiagnosed, I behaved, and suddenly I smiled. I was scared to be categorized, to be stereotyped as a Black silly-angry-non-content woman. Even though I tried to mask it, I wasn't strong enough to do it fully. Anyway, wasn't I supposed to let my guard down for him to see me, to see my condition?

So, beyond all expectations, I gave him a chance – not all white people are the same, so why shouldn't I have given him the benefit of the doubt? He seemed like a nice guy after all.

The fact that this doctor concluded the assessment by saying I had *mild* ADHD made me question how he perceived me. When I told him about my emotional dysregulation, for example when I can be extremely irritated, did he just think, 'Aren't all black women angry?' or when I mentioned my inability to get amazing grades at school despite trying really hard, did he just think, 'Aren't all black people mediocre anyway?'. That, I will never know.

Furthermore, because I present most of the time in a feminine way, but also perhaps because I am Black, people tend to assume I am straight. Let's be honest, the collective consciousness never portrays Black folks when thinking about queerness. In fact, ask someone to close their eyes and imagine in their head a random queer person, then ask them to describe that same person. What is the imaginary queer individual likely to look like? Don't you think that person would be white? Whiteness is the default. Blackness and queerness as a whole lack representation in mainstream media, so no wonder that they would portray a white queer individual.

It always blows my mind when some people cannot see that I am queer. For me it's so obvious, which makes me think that people see me through a different lens, and not how I see myself. It also means that even though I don't like it, I am benefiting from passing. In most situations where I might be surrounded by cis straight lads, where outing myself could be dangerous, I could just not say anything, and they would assume I was also straight. It's safer as a cis queer person, not necessarily as a Black woman. The joy of intersectionality!

So, following the same process, the psychiatrist also assumed the above. He mentioned in the report that my ADHD was affecting my relationships and lately my 'boyfriend'. Hello unconscious bias, long time no see!

If the doctor was able to project heteronormativity on me, why wouldn't he project his anti-Blackness bias too? Not maliciously of course, but the result is the same, isn't it?

Before closing this chapter, I feel the need to clarify one last thing.

Yes, my ADHD has affected my previous relationships and the one with Hector. I went through the assessment because I realized my emotional dysregulation due to the overwhelming situation was affecting others, especially my partner. Nonetheless, while the above was the reason why I got the assessment in first place, I understand that I also needed it for myself.

When researching ADHD prior to my assessment, I understood that having fifty thoughts at a time, getting distracted during conversations, having issues memorizing and feeling overwhelmed in most situations weren't things that everyone experiences, or at least not on the highly impactful and often negative level as me. Recently it had got worse, and it prevented me from sleeping at night, or from falling asleep sometimes.

Everything is intrinsically connected, so if I can manage my symptoms better it will have a positive impact on my relationships, both friendly and romantically.

One of the things I have been attempting is to try to recognize when I feel overwhelmed. That way, I can understand and prevent the feeling of frustration. Easier said than done, though, but oh well, some things take time. I am looking forward to starting my treatment; it should be soon now. I had a call from the GP a couple of days ago saying that my diagnosis had reached the NHS psychiatrists, and they are the ones who will be initiating the treatment. We've almost reached a month now but I can now see the light at the end of the tunnel.

Interlude

My ADHD assessment experience made me think of a poem I wrote last year about anti-Blackness and the mass killing of African Americans.

I wrote it three months before George Floyd's murder and as an honouring piece for Ahmaud Arbery, who got killed on 23rd February 2020 by two white supremacists while he was out jogging. The poem is called *Free at Last*:

FREE AT LAST

They refuse to use the term,

They say white supremacy doesn't exist.

They say not all white people are the same,

We know that, it's systemic.

But they don't know what it feels like to be scared in the daylight.

But they will never fear to be lynched just because they're Black.

So they refuse to say white privilege, they refuse to say white supremacy,

And as a result they subconsciously delay the call for justice

Ahmaud Arbery 25, Trayvon Martin 17, Oscar Grant 22, shot dead, execution style.

How many more lives do you need to finally realize?

So you need to understand this isn't about you as a person,

This is about a system that together WE need to overcome.

So this poem is a call in and a call to action,

Cause together I know we can fight oppression.

Because white voices in the world we live in have 10 times more impact,

They have 10 times more power than Black voices it's a fact.

So use the term to explain, use the term to describe,

Use these words again and again as your weapon to fight.

Because I believe in you and I believe in human rights,

Because the Black Lives Matter movement will have even more power, if you are part of the march.

CHAPTER 4

Intersecting Gender Identity & Blackness

The complexity of intersectionality is that things do not have to be limited; identities or characteristics often mix and coagulate to become an undefined mass. I have myself been questioning my gender lately – after my breakup with Julie, it was like an eye-opener. I then did some research, but I wasn't able to find something matching with how I feel. One of the issues being the lack of representation. I cannot see people out there who look like me: Black femme but who also has this small percentage of something else. The term 'queer' is what fits the most with me but also the term 'woman', which sometimes, on rare occasions, does echo a bit wrongly in my ears when pronounced by some folks. My research led me to agree that being a woman is the part of my gender that is static, therefore my gender identity is aligned with the gender I was assigned at birth. When I came out to myself as queer, it felt obvious to me: the word queer itself vibrated, seduced me, I felt drawn to it. Despite the definition not being crystal clear, it did make sense to me in terms of my sexual identity but also for its political aspect.

Being queer is a controversy. People who look at my dating history are confused; they can't put me in a box, and I like that. I believe that the definition we put behind the word queer is individual. There is not one way to be queer, or one way to describe what it is exactly. I have always known I wasn't straight, because even at the time when I was dating men, I had a few sexual encounters with women between my serious relationships. But at the time, I did not have the knowledge. At the time, I had never heard of the word queer, nor did I fully understand the diversity of identities falling under the rainbow umbrella.

One of the poems I wrote last year talks about being queer. I will share it with you. Let's have another poetry break. If you want to grab some water or anything else, it is now time. Are you ready?

TO BE QUEER

Love, amour, eros.

Does labels are made for all of us?

We often discover ourselves through someone else,

That's how I finally discovered my queerness.

Thinking about my experience, I have always known that I wasn't bi,

Because when I used that word, it didn't fit, I couldn't identify.

To say that I was straight actually I don't know,

Because this label is a special one, applied per default.

Because everyone is heterosexual until proven otherwise,

That's one of the main reasons why we have to go through the struggle of coming out.

Don't you think everything could be way way more easy,

If we didn't assume someone's sexual orientation or gender identity?

But here we are, and so far away from acceptance,

Dreaming of celebration of love, not remembrance.

Even though, we've been pushed aside,

Even if, they want us to think, that this world is not made for us.

Even though they make us comprise,

Even if they refuse to recognize our love.

We resist, we fight back, we thrive, we gather,

We try as much as we can to celebrate one another.

Because our present is with people, cis, trans but also non-binary,

Because we have to celebrate everyone with integrity and because what will be will be.

To be Queer is the acceptance of the other, for who they are or who they aren't yet.

To be Queer it's to know who you are but then forget,

To be Queer it's to be political, to be free, to be everything and nothing at the same time.

To be Queer, it's him, her, them and I.

While I now seem proud, it hasn't always been as easy to be at peace with myself and my queer identity. In fact, for a while, back in France, I would not allow myself to fall in love with a woman. I thought women were good enough for lust but nothing serious. I wanted kids, I wanted a family, and how would I get that if I wasn't in a relationship with a cis man? I was ignorant, and because of my ignorance I have hurt people – casual encounters or dates that could have turned into so much more. I remember apologizing to one of my friends who I had sex with – she wanted us to be together but I was ashamed, and I could not do it. I apologized because I used her – not intentionally, although I did. She was kind enough to forgive me.

The feeling I have now about my gender identity is like the feeling I had before I understood I was queer. I knew something was different, but I could not quite name it.

Ellipsis

However, if I initially intended to talk more about my gender identity, while going back to this section I felt like perhaps it was not the right time.

(My writing process is something else; I haven't been writing the content of each chapter in order. Probably another ADHD thing. So basically, my work was based purely on how inspired I felt in the moment. Which means I am not following a particular order.)

It could be the topic of my next book, maybe – who knows? As I already said, one thing I know for certain is that my breakup with Julie really made me reconsider everything and question myself a lot. If, before, I thought that my queerness was only covering the aspect of my sexuality, I now know that it is more than just that.

Being queer is my identity, on a sexual but also gender aspect – which means that I am more than just my gender. I was assigned female at birth and I would say that I am 99% aligned with the gender I was assigned. Hence, I am self-identifying as a cis-person – it doesn't bother me, and I am cis; it's a fact.

I feel like a woman and I am proud to be one. Nonetheless, I have this 1% left which is neither male nor female. It exists in the absence of gender but is not non-binary. I am not even sure I am making much sense right now, but I hope you can guess what I mean. It is probably as complicated for you to understand as it is for me. When I started questioning, I lost myself in an Internet void of never-ending new tabs opened and terms I had never heard of before. I somehow became this gender identity researcher, and it was mind-blowing but also tiring. Questioning is really tiring! Some of the terminology I found was kind of close to how I feel but not quite:

- ***Demiflux***: *'a gender identity where one part is static, and the other(s) fluctuate(s) in intensity. For example, the static side could* *be female, but the other side could be male. The male part can fluctuate, going from full intensity (male), half intensity (demiboy), to no intensity (agender), while the female part does not fluctuate. It is similar to demigender in which the gender is almost 'split in two' or divided into two sections. The difference is that demiflux has a part that fluctuates.'*[7]

- ***Aporagender**: 'a non-binary gender, or group of genders, defined as being separate from male, female, and anything in between, while still being a strong and specific gendered feeling. Aporagender people are not a combination of male and female (androgyne), and still have a strong gendered feeling, unlike agender.'*[8]
- ***Girlflux**: 'a gender identity in which a person can experience varying degrees of female identity, despite their biological sex. For example, one could feel 0% (agender), 50% (demigirl), 100% (woman), or anything in between such as paragirl and librafeminine. The intensity can fluctuate over any period of time.'*[9]
- ***Paragender**: 'the feeling very near one gender and partially something else which keeps you from feeling fully that gender. Similar in definition to perigender and offgender. Paragender people are in the range of feeling 51-99% of a connection to another gender.'*[10]

Despite having some similarities to how I see myself, the above terms did not fit. Queer is the only word I have been able to

---

7 https://gender.wikia.org/wiki/Demiflux

8 https://lgbta.wikia.org/wiki/Aporagender

9 https://gender.wikia.org/wiki/Girlflux

10 https://gender.wikia.org/wiki/Paragender

identify as. It is such a powerful word while also being undefined. It can expand but also shrinks, in order to be what you want it to be. Queer is my home, queer fits me like a glove. Queer was love at first sight. Queer is a feeling that forever lasts. Queer is worn with pride and so I am as a Queer Black woman.

You Are Now Reaching the End of the Book

If this book is a user guide to support both white and Black people in their romantic relationships or in their relationships in general. It is also a self-empowerment tool for Black people. The aim is to celebrate Black individuals. It is an ode to self-love and compassion. I wish this book to be a warm support for uneasy days, a reminder to be unapologetically Black and proud.

I wish to provide the comfort I have found reading or watching content produced by Black folks celebrating Blackness. This content makes me feel seen, and understood even, when sometimes I do not understand myself. I wish this book to be a reminder that you, we are not alone.

I have just finished watching *Ma Rainey's Black Bottom* on Netflix, an inspiring drama film directed by George C Wolfe, written by Ruben Santiago-Hudson, based on a play by August Wilson, starring the amazing Viola Davis as Ma Rainey herself and Chadwick Boseman (RIP).

The story of the radical Mother of the Blues grew on me. I also watched the documentary, and I am currently listening to her music. It got me inspired to write, because like this movie, I want this book to be a legacy for Black folks, a reminder that we exist and have always been. Not only through pain, but also through talents like Ma Rainey at the time, but also through talented actresses like Viola Davis and Chadwick Boseman. We need to know those people; we need to say their names and pass them on. We do have so many talents in the Black community who are not celebrated enough, compared to their white counterparts. In terms of the intersection of Blackness and queerness, there is no need to go far or mainstream to also find truly impactful individuals. In fact, in the Brighton queer community, I can find several folks, but I'd like to share one name especially. This person is a true source of inspiration. Her name is Kuchenga.

In February this year, I got the opportunity to pass on a message on BBC radio as part of LGBTQ History Month. I had to talk about who I am inspired by and the person who came straight to my mind was her. Here is what I shared with BBC Radio listeners: 'I am inspired by Kuchenga because she makes me feel I belong. She is the first Black woman I heard talking openly about colourism at an event for Black people only I went to four years ago. She brought the subject in such an easy manner, that it almost felt natural and somehow totally fine to talk about it. I that moment she put words on something I had been thinking for a while but wasn't able to describe or understand. I am forever grateful to have a dark-skinned woman I can look up to, who also happens to be an amazing, kind, pure and friendly soul.' If you don't know Kuchenga Shenje, she is a writer and journalist, and she has contributed to *Gal-Dem*, *British Vogue*, *Harper Bazaar* and much more. It's worth checking her work out so give her name a Google search.

While you are on Google, you can also check out Tarik Elmoutawakil, who is an artist, producer and event manager, thanks to whom I realized one of my dreams. Back in 2017 (I think it was), I had the chance to see Alok Vaid-Menon perform on stage at the Marlborough Theatre in Brighton. Tarik also curated an astonishing Afro-futurist event called *Brownton Abbey*, which was held in the Brighton Dome (a huge achievement in terms of reclaiming the space by Black and Brown folks!!) in 2018. I would like to add a couple of names to your list. The first one being Ven Paldano, who co-created QTIPOC Brighton which has positively affected the community. Also Ellis J. Johnson[11], who besides being a wonderful human being is also a trained counsellor for trans, queer and questioning people. Ellis has several times used his skills to support the queer community during this complicated time.

Unfortunately, Brighton is not what you would call a racially diverse city. If you narrow down from people of color to Black folks with a dark skin and queer on top of that, I am afraid you won't find lot of us.

This was one of the reasons why I thought several times about moving to London. However, the busyness of this town is making it nearly impossible for me to live there. Too crowded, too big, too much. I like having the option to go to town without having to take the bus or an Uber. Being away from big cities and living by the sea has definitely had a positive impact on my mental health.

---

11 https://www.transcounselling.co.uk/

Perhaps once everything re-opens, we will notice that more Black queer folks have moved from London to Brighton during the pandemic. I know for a fact that lot of Londoners did move here during lockdown, because who wants to live in a capital when everything that is making a big city interesting is closed? To be continued…

To conclude, this book is the results of years of self-reflection combined with my past and actual experiences dating white folks. It is not a unique model of how interracial relationships works, nor a guide that will miraculously solve all the problems in your relationship. Perhaps you are Black and queer, in an interracial couple, and you are not suffering from anti-ness within the limit of this relationship and that's great! Or perhaps you do and you can relate to my experience too. If that's the case, I hope this book was able help you a bit, perhaps even to find your voice and empower yourself. This book can also be used as a tool to educate your partner or friends, without you having to put the energy in yourself. Either way, I hope you have enjoyed reading it as much as I enjoyed writing it.

Last Interlude

Genderless Menstrual Leave Campaign

I have been working lately on a campaign to request the UK government to adopt a new Genderless Menstrual Leave.

We are not asking for much, only **1 day per month** therefore **12 days per year** of leave for people who bleed regardless of their gender.

The aims are to:

- *Support individuals who have chronic pain due to menstruation, especially but not only for individuals experiencing dysmenorrhea, endometriosis, ovarian cyst and other conditions making menstruation painful.*
- *Break stigma around menstruation, promote gender equality and recognise genders as a spectrum. Implement an inclusive policy that is not centring cisgenderism or the binary men/women.*

SPECIFICATIONS

Not a 'women only' menstrual leave. For any person who has menstrual cycles regardless of their gender. Therefore this leave does also apply to non-binary and transgender individuals.

PROPOSAL

- ***The individual can decide to opt in or out****, by opting in the employee will have a minimum of 12 extra days allowance added to their sick leave balance.*
- ***Non-disclosure agreement & disclaimer****. To mitigate the risk of discrimination at work, the nature of the leave should be disclosed by the employee only and at their discretion. This measure will prevent trans and non-binary individuals from being outed at work and ensure anonymity. Depending on the company policy a disclaimer should be signed at the opt-in stage. The Genderless Menstrual Leave allowance should be named Special Leave or remain unnamed and be added to the overall employee sickness allowance.*

Reminder: no one should be discriminated against based on protected characteristics such as 'sex' or 'gender reassignment' as per Equality Act 2010.

We need exposure to raise awareness about the campaign and get people to sign the petition. The more signatures we get the closer we are to getting the government to review the proposal!

A few milestones: we were lucky enough to get the attention of Rain Dove (model and activist) who offered us a live interview on Instagram! We also had an Instagram takeover with Anti-Diet Riot Club, Mermaids UK retweeted us and *DIVA* magazine also shared and wrote an article about the initiative[12].

You want to support the campaign?

Sign the petition!! The petition was set up on change.org under the name ***'Adopt a new Genderless Menstrual Leave'***[13] but also write about the campaign and share it on social media. Thank you!

---

12 https://divamag.co.uk/2021/02/16/new-campaign-launched-in-support-of-genderless-menstrual-leave/

13 https://www.change.org/p/boris-johnson-adopt-a-new-genderless-menstrual-leave

Aftermath

When I started this book, Hector and I had broken up and were supposed to meet up to talk things through. We did do that. They came to mine a couple of days ago. I haven't felt that way in years – this breakup was horrible. I lost my appetite and I lost 4 kilos in the space of a week. I was not able to sleep the whole night without waking up to then find myself sobbing for hours. If the above was not clear enough, I can say that yes, I had a hard time.

So, they came, we talked, and I initially thought they did not wish for us to get back together because they mentioned via text a few days before we met up that they were trying to move on.

During the discussion, they explained me how they felt, and so did I. We finally arrived at a common agreement that we had rushed into things, that we needed things to change for sure if we wanted to continue. We both realized even more that we could not spend our lives without each other. This was comforting. I even tried to go on Tinder a few days after the breakup and I could not even do it. I installed the app and found myself crying then deleted it straight away.

So, after this long discussion, we finally got back together in October last year.

Ellipsis

When I am writing this now, it is six months later. Things are different to how they were when I started writing the aftermath. While we've managed to have a great time together, we do struggle to come out stronger from arguments. It often feels like we are making three steps forward and then ten steps back, which is not healthy. It's hard because since the day I met them three years ago, I instantly felt like they were the person I could see myself spending my life with. So, I wish we could understand how to make this work.

Agreeing to disagree is one thing that we need to embrace for sure. Sometimes in an argument no one is right or wrong – sometimes we both are. First and foremost, it is not a competition, there is no prize to win and no one will be crowned at the end of the fight. Therefore, unless we are discussing an important matter, I think that we should learn to let things slide and just agree to disagree, without overthinking it. Without overreacting or thinking in a narrow and binary way that because we are not aligned on (insignificant) stuff, we are not meant to be together. As a French person, I am more likely to be fine with disagreements, which for me aren't arguments. I am usually fine with them, as long as the matter is unimportant – so, for example, when we are not talking about race. Though I am not as cool as I seem, and all the above pieces of advice for my relationships are also reminders for myself.

To close this book, I am going to leave you with a last poem I wrote for Hector back in 2018. It has no title:

I had the chance to fall asleep and wake up next to you,

If that's all we can afford then that will do.

Because even if it was short, even if it flew by,

For one moment the world stopped spinning around.

But now you are gone,

You left your smell on my pillow but the bedsheets are cold.

Your perfume is the only thing you left behind,

Your smell and some memories from another kind.

The sea is calmer tonight than it was when I woke up this morning,

Waves are gentle but powerful at the same time.

Little by little they are reaching the edge.

By the time they'll reach the rocks they'll already disappear,

Like my feelings for you, they're on their path to fade away.

Thank you to…

Hope for unintentionally inspiring me to write this book. My neighbor who will recognize herself. Jude for being my endless supporter but also for all your help running my campaigns. Géffie: Effie and Gigi for being such great friends. Noé for the strong friendship despite the distance, and for the help getting my head around ADHD. Kharina for always being proud of me. Arnaud for friendship and support especially during breakups! *DIVA* magazine for believing in the Genderless Menstrual Leave campaign and publishing an article about it. And all the rest.

www.ingramcontent.com/pod-product-compliance
Ingram Content Group UK Ltd.
Pitfield, Milton Keynes, MK11 3LW, UK
UKHW021651190726
13853UKWH00001B/187